It was a sunny day. Sid was playing under the shade of the banyan tree in his neighborhood. None of his friends were home. Avi was at math class, Rohu was at karate, and Praneet was at piano. Classes, classes, classes.

Sid hated being alone. Oh, how he wished that his friends were back!

As he sat on the grass, moping, he heard a **rustling** noise. Then, a giggle.

Sid looked up and found a girl swinging on the branches of the tree. He had never seen her before. Had she just moved here? he wondered. Curious, he called up to her. "Hi, I'm Sid."

The girl hopped down and dusted her hands. Smiling, she said, "I'm Maya."

"I haven't seen you before. Are you new here?" asked Sid.

"Yes," said Maya. "My family and I just moved here a few days ago."

Wow! A new friend thought Sid. He loved meeting new people, and Maya seemed friendly.

"Do you want to play with me?" asked Sid.
"Sure! What do you want to play?" asked Maya.

Sid thought for a moment. "Hide and seek?"
"No," said Maya. "It's no fun with only two people."

"Okay, do you want to play chor police

Or have a running race?".

"Okay! Let's have a race. Where to?" asked Maya.
"First one to touch the wall wins!" yelled Sid as he took off.

Both of them ran as hard as they could. They touched the wall at the same time and cried out, "I win!"
"I won!" said Maya, crossly.
"No, I won!" replied Sid.
"I was much faster! I didn't even see you running next to me," huffed Maya.
"Humph... I still think I won..." Sid said.

Tired, they sat down next to each other.
Sid looked at Maya and noticed her fixing something behind her ears.

"What is that?" he asked, pointing to it.

Maya answered, "These are my cochlear implants. They started to fall off when I was running, so I had to put them back on."

"Co... what?" asked Sid.
"Cochlear implants. They help me hear," Maya said.

Sid was very curious. He started asking Maya lots of questions.

"How did you get them? How does that piece stay on your head? What happens when you take it off? What do you mean they

What-"

"Slow down!" said Maya, laughing. "Let me tell you about them."

How does that piece stay on your head?
Does it hurt?
When did you get them?
What happens when you take it off?

"When I was born, I couldn't hear. I started wearing hearing aids to **make sounds louder.**"

"Like speakers in your ears?" asked Sid.
"Um... I think so," said Maya.

"So then why do you need this 'coco' thing?" Sid asked. "Shouldn't the hearing aids help you hear just fine?"

"Well, the doctors found out I had profound hearing loss. I couldn't hear people talking or things making noise. I could maybe hear an aeroplane if I was right next to it. Hearing aids were only helping me hear sometimes. So that's when I had a surgery to get my cochlear implants."

"So now do your ears work like mine?" Sid asked.

"Well, I guess they work almost like your ears," said Maya. "But for me, a microphone is what the sound goes into. Then, the cochlear implants help sounds get from my ear to my brain."

"So it's like a taxi service for sound to get around?" asked Sid.

"That's right! My mom tells me that **the brain is the thing that is listening**.

The ears just hear the sounds but the brain understands them!" said Maya. "I need cochlear implants so the sound can get to my brain."

"Oh! I understand now. But I don't get how they stick to your head."

Maya said, "I had a surgery to put a magnet inside my head. The part of the earpiece that is outside has another magnet in it. I just bring them together and they stick!"

"Wow! That's so cool!" said Sid.

Maya **beamed** with pride.

"I also went to a doctor and found out that I can't see very well with just my eyes," said Sid. "That's why I **need these glasses!**"

"So how do your glasses work?" Maya asked.

"Hm... I don't know," said Sid. "But if I don't wear them I can't see very well."

"Just like I can't hear if I don't wear my implants!" said Maya.

"Hey Maya, can I touch your cochlear implant?" asked Sid.

"Sure!" said Maya. "But only if you let me try your glasses on!"

"Okay, but you have to be very careful," said Sid. "I already broke one pair this year!"

Sid gave her his glasses, and Maya gave him her cochlear implant.

Maya tried them on and said, "Everything's so blurry! I can barely see."

Laughing, Sid exclaimed, "That's how I feel without them!"

Maya gave Sid his glasses back. "Much better!" he said.

Maya heard some kids cheering at a distance. "Hey, 

hear that?" she asked. "It sounds like some kids playing!"

"Oh! Those are my friends Rohan, Avinash, and Praneet!" said Sid. "They must be back from their classes. Do you want to go play with them?"

"Okay!" said Maya. Just like Sid, she liked meeting new people. "Let's go!" she said.

And they both ran off together.

About Hearing Loss

- Out of every 1000 babies, 3-6 babies are born deaf.
- Childhood deafness can have a negative impact on learning to speak and understanding what is being said.
- When hearing loss is diagnosed early and children receive timely intervention, they can learn to listen, speak, go to school, get jobs, and live independent, productive lives.

About Hearing Technology & Intervention

- Children as young as a month old can be tested for hearing loss.
- Hearing technology like hearing aids, cochlear implants, and bone anchored hearing devices can help children hear the language(s) around them.
- Families can help children who are deaf or hard of hearing to learn to listen and speak with support from teachers, therapists, speech language pathologists, audiologists, listening and spoken language specialists.
- Many different communication options are available to children who are deaf or hard of hearing, and their families. Some choose spoken language, some choose to sign, and some use a combination of the two, or additional supports like cued speech. Ultimately, what matters is that children who are deaf or hard of hearing have the communication skills to express their needs, wants, thoughts, and opinions.

Listening Together is a not for profit organization that supports the education and rehabilitation of children who are deaf and hard of hearing around the world through parent empowerment, professional development, and public awareness.

Parent Empowerment

Parents and family members of children who are deaf or hard of hearing, who are learning to listen and speak can participate in individual or group tele-intervention sessions. In these sessions parents receive information about hearing loss and hearing technology, along with strategies to develop spoken language(s).

Professional Development

Speech language pathologists, teachers of students who are deaf or hard of hearing, early interventionists, audiologists, and mainstream teachers can develop their knowledge and skills related to auditory-verbal practice, listening and spoken language intervention by participating in online courses and individual mentoring.

Public Awareness

Awareness within parents, professionals, and communities about the impact of hearing loss and how they can provide support is crucial for positive long-term outcomes. Our free monthly webinars, blog posts, and other resources are available to all.

Learn more about Listening Together at **www.listeningtogether.com**

About the Co-Founders of Listening Together

Uma Soman, PhD, LSLS Cert AVEd.

Uma Soman is a teacher of students who are deaf or hard of hearing (DHH), and Listening and Spoken Language Specialist Auditory Verbal Educator. She has been working with children who are DHH, their families, and professionals for more than 15 years. As Director of Professional Development, Uma develops courses on listening and spoken language intervention, and trains speech language pathologists, audiologists, teachers of DHH students, and mainstream teachers. She mentors professionals pursuing Listening and Spoken Language Specialist Certification.

Ahladhini Rao Dugar, M.E.D.

Ahladhini Rao Dugar is an early interventionist and teacher of the students who are deaf or hard of hearing. She has been working with families of children who are DHH for more than 15 years in the United States and India. As Director of Parent Empowerment, Ahladhini works with families and professionals from varied socio-economic, cultural, and linguistic backgrounds. She provides early intervention services for children who are DHH and family-centered coaching.

About the Author

Akhand Dugar

Akhand is a high schooler from the Bay Area in California. This book, his first, is inspired by his experience as a hearing child in a school for the deaf or hard of hearing. Today, he is a part of his school's newspaper and an active volunteer in his community. Akhand loves to read, go on road trips, and explore new foods and places. He is currently working on the second and third installments in the Maya and Sid series.

About the Artist

Swati Namjoshi

Swati is a visual artist and counselor from Pune, India. Her content label 'StudioMo' talks about empathy, inclusion, and more. It's no surprise that the Listening Together team, their efforts, and Maya's story jumped right into her art and heart.

Swati is all set to dive right into the next story, the second book in the Maya and Sid series.

Made in the USA
Middletown, DE
08 August 2021

45620647R00018